# Face Painting

Written by Patricia Silver (Patty the Clown)
Illustrated by Louise Phillips

KIDS CAN PRESS

For John-Michael (Peeper the Clown)—
My son, my student, my teacher, my inspiration
and my friend.

## Acknowledgments

Applause for the young stars who appeared in the book:
John-Michael, Erika, Bryan, Rashan, Aiden, Roxanne,
Kiera, Madelene and Erik. Thanks to artistic consultants
Carolanne Maclean, Picasso Painters (Georgia Steel), Pamela Hammond,
Angela Minaker, Kristin Scythes and Koo Koo the Clown (Kim Cayer).
Special appreciation for the patience and support of the
Sphere Entertainment staff and Tim Phillips.
And a big clown salute to Dandy the Clown (Dan Stapleton),
who inspired the creation of Patty the Clown.

KIDS CAN DO IT and the 📖 logo are trademarks of
Kids Can Press Ltd.

Kids Can Press acknowledges the financial support of the
Government of Canada, through the BPIDP, for our
publishing activity.

Published in Canada by
Kids Can Press Ltd.
29 Birch Avenue
Toronto, ON  M4V 1E2

Published in the U.S. by
Kids Can Press Ltd.
2250 Military Road
Tonawanda, NY 14150

Edited by Laurie Wark
Designed by Karen Powers
Photography by Frank Baldassarra
Printed in Hong Kong by Wing King Tong Company Limited

The hard cover edition of this book is smyth sewn
casebound.
The paperback edition fo this book is limp sewn with a
drawn-on cover.

CM 00  0 9 8 7 6 5 4 3 2
CM PA 00  0 9 8 7 6 5 4 3 2 1

**Canadian Cataloguing in Publication Data**

Silver, Patricia
    Face painting

(Kids can do it)
ISBN 1-55074-845-9 (bound)    ISBN 1-55074-689-8 (pbk.)

1. Face painting — Juvenile literature. I. Phillips, Louise.
II. Title. III. Series.

TT911.S54 2000      j745.5      C99-933034-9

Kids Can Press is a Nelvana company

# Contents

# Introduction

*You can become your favorite character with face paints and simple costume pieces. In this book, you'll find lots of ideas for faces, costumes and activities. Face painting is safe, easy and fun. Using face paint instead of a mask means that you can always see clearly. You can draw simple or fancy designs. Paints can be used to make "tattoos" on your hands, arms or feet. You can become one of the stars in this book, or use your imagination to think up a personality and its design. It's best to have someone else paint your face, so paint with a friend and take turns. Costumes can be homemade or store-bought. You can put together your own dress-up box by gathering costume pieces from garage sales or old clothes. Have a good time!*

## MATERIALS

Gather all materials before you begin.

- pots of face paints or face-painting crayons. Grease paint lasts the longest, but water-based paints are less messy and easier to put on and take off. Costume shops and some gift or specialty stores sell paints in a kit or a palette, which is an economical way to buy them.

- a table covered in plastic or newspaper and a chair for each child
- water for washing brushes and for mixing with paint

- a mirror on a stand

- old towels, rags or paper towels

- paintbrushes in different sizes. Cotton swabs can sometimes be used instead of brushes.

- facial tissues

- makeup sponges

- extra-fine glitter

- skin moisturizer and cold cream if you are using grease paints

- a black makeup or eyebrow pencil

- household items to outline shapes, such as a lipstick tube, the lid from a baby-food jar, plastic cookie cutters or stencils

- hair clips and elastics for holding the hair off your face while you're painting

- an oversized T-shirt or big towel to use as a smock over your clothes

# Face-painting tips

1. Put on your costume, then put a smock, big T-shirt or towel over it.

2. Start with a clean face. Pick a design from this book or create your own.

3. If you have long hair, hold it back with a hair clip or elastic.

4. Spread a little moisturizer all over your face if you're using grease paints.

5. To color the entire face, dip a small sponge into a pot of color or rub the face-painting crayon onto the sponge, then spread the makeup over the face. Use a damp sponge with water-based face paints.

6. Let the paint dry for at least three minutes if you're using water-based face paints. Grease paint never dries completely.

7. If necessary, draw the outline of the design on the face with a black makeup pencil or face-painting crayon.

8. Paint the design features inside the black outlines with the crayons or brushes. The paint should have a creamy consistency. You may have to paint over the color twice to make it brighter. You can blend colors to make new ones, such as white and red to make pink. Remember to rinse your brushes and sponges between colors.

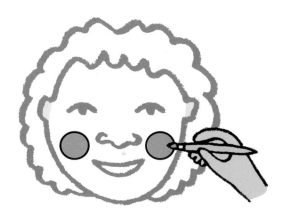

**9.** If you wish, use your finger or a cotton swab to lightly dab small amounts of glitter on your cheeks (the glitter will stick to wet makeup).

**10.** Make freckles or other features using the black makeup pencil on the dry paint. You can color your lips with face paint or lipstick.

**11.** Admire yourself in the mirror!

## SAFETY

• To test if you are allergic to the face paints, paint a small patch on the inside of your arm. Let it dry for at least ten minutes, then wash it off. If your skin turns red, don't use the paints. You can create your character with the costume ideas in this book.

• Keep the brushes and glitter away from your eyes. If your entire face is being painted, be careful not to smudge the paint into your eyes.

• Store the paints and brushes away from children under three years old.

## CLEAN-UP

**1.** Tissue any glitter off first.

**2.** Remove water-based paints by washing your face with mild soap and water. Remove grease paint by spreading cold cream on your face and wiping it off with a tissue.

**3.** Put the makeup back in its container and close it tightly.

# Mime

*This clown is silent, but communicates with hand, face and body movements.*

## YOU WILL NEED

- white, red and black face paints or face-painting crayons
- face-painting supplies (see pages 4 – 5)
- glitter (optional)

1 Use a sponge to paint the whole face white. Let it dry for three minutes.

2 Paint a small red mouth.

3 Paint a long black line down from each eyebrow to the middle of each cheek. Paint a black dot at the bottom of each line. Dab glitter on the dots, if you like.

4 Paint black eyebrows in the middle of the forehead.

## EASY COSTUME PIECES

- a white leotard
- a black turtleneck and tights
- a striped T-shirt
- white gloves

## MORE MIME FUN

Silently act out words or stories. Pretend to climb a wall, step over a large rock or open a door. These are traditional mime moves.

# Hobo

*This clown looks sad, but can be very funny. You may see the hobo at the circus.*

## YOU WILL NEED

- white, red and black face paints or face-painting crayons
- a black makeup pencil or face-painting crayon
- hair gel (optional)
- face-painting supplies (see pages 4 – 5)

1 Sponge a light layer of white over the whole face. Let the paint dry for three minutes.

2 Paint a red circle on the end of the nose.

3 Smudge black paint on the cheeks and chin.

4 Outline a sad black mouth and paint it red.

5 Draw three sides of a rectangle over each eyebrow and fill them with gray paint (blend white and black to make gray).

6 Draw a black cross under each eye.

7 Put hair gel in your hair to make it stick out of a hat.

## EASY COSTUME PIECES

- patched or ripped pants with suspenders
- an old floppy hat
- a bandanna
- a long stick with a satchel tied to it
- a rumpled shirt with a pillow under it to fill out your stomach

# Peeper

*This neat white face is the most common clown style. Watch your face light up when you smile!*

## YOU WILL NEED

- white, red and blue face paints or face-painting crayons
- a black makeup pencil or face-painting crayon
- face-painting supplies (see pages 4 – 5)
- glitter (optional)

**1** Use a sponge to paint the whole face white. Let it dry for three minutes.

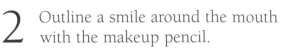

**2** Outline a smile around the mouth with the makeup pencil.

**3** Outline a quarter-moon on each cheek.

4 Draw a triangle over each eyebrow.

5 Outline a circle on the end of the nose. Outline the eyes, if you like.

6 Color the quarter-moons purple (blend red and blue to make purple).

7 Color the triangles blue.

8 Color the mouth and nose circle red.

9 Dab glitter on the cheeks and nose, if you like.

## OTHER IDEAS

To paint Patty's clown face (on the back cover of this book), change the quarter-moons on the cheeks to red circles and the triangles to blue half-moons. Add freckles with a black makeup pencil.

## EASY COSTUME PIECES

- a colorful hat with a flower pinned to it
- a wild-colored long tie
- bright ribbons for hair ties
- a colorful shirt or T-shirt

# Cat

*You'll look purrrfect as this cat, or you can change the base color to become a marmalade cat or a gray tabby (blend red and yellow to make orange, or black and white to make gray).*

## YOU WILL NEED

- white and black face paint or face painting crayon
- a black makeup pencil
- glitter (optional)
- face-painting supplies (see pages 4 – 5)

1 Sponge a light layer of white on the whole face. Let the paint dry for three minutes.

2 For the nose and lips, draw two triangles on top of each other with the points meeting under the nose.

3 Paint the lips black.

**4** Put black dots above the upper lip.

**5** Paint whiskers with a makeup pencil or brush by making three short lines on each cheek.

**6** Outline each eye in black, making the lines stretch to the edge of the face.

**7** Add black lines over the eyebrows pointing to the temples.

**8** Dab glitter on the nose and whiskers, if you like.

## OTHER IDEAS

Turn the cat into a mouse by using brown instead of white paint. Make round ears to wear or try painting ears right onto the face.

## EASY COSTUME PIECES

- a leotard or turtleneck and leggings
- a headband with felt or fun-fur ears attached
- a long piece of fabric or fun fur pinned on for a tail
- gloves for paws

# Dalmatian dog

*Turn this dog into a brown dog by painting a brown face with white spots.*

## YOU WILL NEED

- white, black and red face paints or face-painting crayons
- a black makeup pencil or face-painting crayon
- face painting supplies (see pages 4 – 5)

1 Use a sponge to paint the whole face white. Let it dry for three minutes.

2 Outline a tongue hanging down from the mouth, and paint it red.

3 Paint a black nose and mouth with a triangle joining them.

4 Add black dots between the nose and mouth.

6 Paint large black spots on the face.

5 Paint a long black "S" on each side of the face starting at the eyebrow and ending at the mouth.

## EASY COSTUME PIECES

- black or white pants, sweatpants, pyjamas or leggings, and a white shirt
- a long piece of fabric for a tail, pinned to the pants
- a headband with ears made out of black and white felt
- black or white mittens for paws
- black felt patches stitched, pinned or fabric glued onto a shirt

# Rabbit

*Get a small bunch of carrots as a prop,
and hop to it!*

## YOU WILL NEED

- white and red face paints
  or face-painting crayons
- a black makeup pencil, paint
  or face-painting crayon
- glitter (optional)
- face-painting supplies (see pages 4 – 5)

1 Sponge the whole face pink
  (blend white and red to make pink).
  Let the paint dry for three minutes.

2 Outline a tall half-moon over each
  eye with the makeup pencil or
  black paint.

3 Color a darker pink inside the
  half-moons.

4 Paint a small red patch on the nose. Dab on some glitter, if you like.

5 Outline big cheeks with the makeup pencil or black paint. Start at the nose, go around each cheek and down to the mouth. Color the cheeks white.

6 Use the pencil to draw curved lines as whiskers inside the cheeks.

7 Draw a black triangle with a point in the middle above the lip.

8 Draw big teeth on the chin. Paint them white.

## EASY COSTUME PIECES

- a headband with two long, pink felt ears
- fuzzy white or pink pajamas, turtleneck or sweatshirt and leggings
- a white or pink leotard and tights
- white gloves or mittens for paws
- a large powder puff, pompom or cotton-ball tail pinned to the costume

# Lion

*Add a crown and have some roaring good fun as king or queen of the jungle!*

## YOU WILL NEED

- yellow, red, green and black face paints or face-painting crayons
- a black makeup pencil or face-painting crayon
- face-painting supplies (see pages 4 – 5)

**1** Sponge the whole face yellow. Let the paint dry for three minutes.

**2** Paint light brown ovals around the edges of the face (blend red and green to make brown). Paint lines coming from each oval.

**3** Paint a black nose and lips with a triangle joining them.

**4** Draw black dots above the mouth with the makeup pencil.

**5** Add whiskers by painting black lines out from the edges of the dots.

**6** Paint bushy dark brown eyebrows.

**7** Paint a black line under each eye and beside each eyebrow.

## EASY COSTUME PIECES

- a yellow T-shirt or turtleneck
- yellow or brown leggings or pants
- use hair gel to make the hair stick out in a wild mane
- make a construction-paper crown
- a brown fabric tail with a yellow pompom on the end

**Why don't lions eat clowns?**

**Because they taste funny!**

# Butterfly

*Make some antennae and wings,*

*and flutter by.*

## YOU WILL NEED

- yellow, blue, white and red face paints or face-painting crayons
- a black makeup pencil or face-painting crayon
- glitter (optional)
- face-painting supplies (see pages 4 – 5)

1 Outline wings with the makeup pencil on each cheek and around each eye, meeting at the nose.

2 Draw a double black line down the center of the nose, between the wings. Add antennae with dots on the end.

3 Fill in the double line with yellow.

**4** Choose a different color for each half of the wing and fill them in. Let the paint dry for three minutes.

**5** Paint thin yellow stripes from the edge of each wing to about halfway to the middle.

**6** Dab circles of glitter in the center of each wing, if you like.

## EASY COSTUME PIECES

- For wings, cut two squares the length of your arm from see-through fabric, chiffon or gauze. Pin or sew one end of each piece to the shoulder of a leotard, T-shirt or girl's bathing suit. Tie the other end to your wrist with long ribbons.

- Make antennae by wrapping aluminum foil balls around the ends of two pipe cleaners. Attach them to a headband.

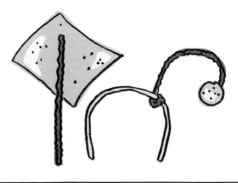

# Witch

*Scrunch up your nose and mouth to look
mean, or smile and be the good witch.*

## YOU WILL NEED

- green, white, black and red face paints
  or face-painting crayons
- a black makeup pencil or
  face-painting crayon
- face-painting supplies (see pages 4 – 5)

1 Sponge the whole face light green
(blend green and white to make
light green). Let the paint dry for three
minutes.

2 Paint black fuzzy eyebrows.

3 Paint the lips black.

**4** Paint a thin red line around the black lips. Add tiny black lines over the lips.

**5** Draw fine black wrinkle lines on each side of the nose, on the forehead and chin, and around the eyes and mouth.

**6** Smudge a little black paint under each cheek.

**7** Paint a black line under each eye.

**8** Paint a small black circle on the nose for a wart.

## EASY COSTUME PIECES

- a black long-sleeved leotard or turtleneck. Sew or pin jagged strips of black fabric to the bottom of the sleeves.
- black tights, leggings or skirt
- a black shawl
- a black construction-paper hat
- a broom

# Skeleton

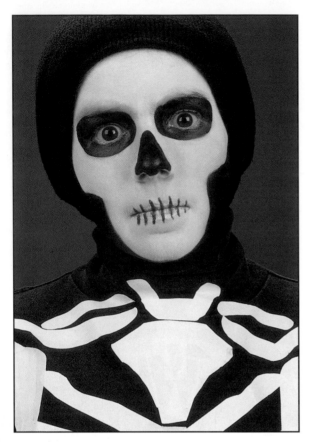

*Dangle your arms to let your
bones hang loose.*

### YOU WILL NEED

- white and black face paints
  or face-painting crayons
- a black makeup pencil or
  face-painting crayon
- face-painting supplies (see pages 4 – 5)

1 Sponge the whole face white
  including the lips. Let the paint
dry for three minutes.

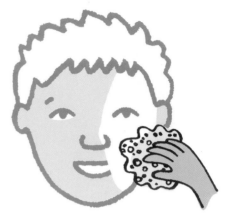

2 Draw a black line from the edges
  of the face across the cheekbones
and down under the chin. Fill outside
the line with black paint.

3 Paint a black circle around
  each eye.

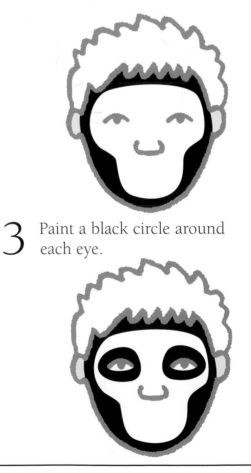

**4** Paint black teeth over the lips.

**5** Paint the whole nose black.

## EASY COSTUME PIECES

- a black hooded robe
- a black leotard and tights with strips of white adhesive tape, crepe paper or fabric pinned or sewn on the leotard to look like bones

Why wouldn't the skeleton cross the road?

Because he had no guts!

# Dr. Frankenstein's monster

*This creature walks with stiff arms and legs.*

## YOU WILL NEED

- green, white, black and red face paints or face-painting crayons
- a black makeup pencil or face-painting crayon
- face-painting supplies (see pages 4 – 5)

1 Sponge the whole face light green (blend green and white to make light green). Let the paint dry for three minutes.

2 Paint black lips.

3 Paint a crooked red line of blood from the top of the forehead to above one eye.

4 Paint black in the hollow of each eye.

5 Paint a thin red line under each eye.

6 Smudge a little black paint just below each cheekbone and across the forehead.

7 Paint a scar on one cheek (see page 39).

8 Paint thick black eyebrows.

## EASY COSTUME PIECES

- an old suit jacket and pants
- hockey or football shoulder pads to wear under the suit
- use eyelash adhesive to attach painted bottle corks to the neck for bolts

# Count Dracula

*This vampire speaks with an accent.*

## YOU WILL NEED

- white, black and red face paints or face-painting crayons
- hair gel (optional)
- a black makeup pencil or face-painting crayon
- face-painting supplies (see pages 4 – 5)

1 Slick hair back with hair gel or water.

2 Sponge a light layer of white over the whole face. Let the paint dry for three minutes.

3 Draw a triangle down from the hairline to above the nose, and paint it black.

**4** Paint a thin red line under each eye.

**5** Paint pointy black eyebrows.

**6** Put a little gray paint on the eyelids and cheeks (blend black and white to make gray).

**7** Paint the lips red.

**8** Paint blood dripping from the edges of the mouth with thin lines of red.

## EASY COSTUME PIECES

- a white shirt
- black pants
- a black cape
- white gloves
- a black bow tie

# Princess

*Throw a ball for your friends
with royal treats.*

## YOU WILL NEED

- blue, white and red face paints
  or face-painting crayons
- a black makeup pencil
- glitter (optional)
- face-painting supplies (see pages 4 – 5)

**1** Put light blue over the eyelids (blend blue and white to make light blue).

**2** Draw big eyelashes under each eye with the makeup pencil.

**3** Paint circles of pink on the cheeks (blend red and white to make pink). Dab glitter on each cheek, if you like.

**4** Paint the lips bright red.

## EASY COSTUME PIECES

- costume jewelry and
  fancy hair ornaments
- a cape and dress gloves
- a construction-paper tiara
  decorated with glitter or sequins

# Pirate

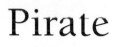

*Arrr, me hearties — lead me to your treasure.*

## YOU WILL NEED

- red, black and white face paints or face-painting crayons
- a black makeup pencil or crayon
- face-painting supplies (see pages 4 – 5)

**1** Draw a bushy mustache and one bushy eyebrow with the makeup pencil or black paint.

**2** Make an eye patch by painting a black circle around one eye and a line from each side of it to the hair.

**3** Dab black paint on the lower part of the cheeks and chin to look like a beard.

**4** Paint a scar on one cheek (see page 39).

### EASY COSTUME PIECES

- a white shirt or striped T-shirt with a sash
- a black vest and black pants
- a bandanna and costume jewelry
- a cardboard sword

# Alien

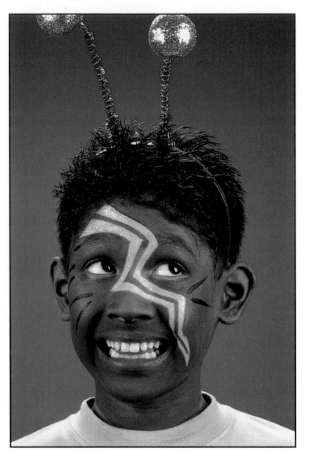

*Invent a language for this visitor.*

## YOU WILL NEED

- yellow, red and blue face paints or face-painting crayons
- a black makeup pencil, paint or face-painting crayon
- glitter (optional)
- hair gel (optional)
- face-painting supplies (see pages 4 – 5)

1 Sponge purple paint on the whole face (blend red and blue to make purple). Let the paint dry for three minutes.

2 Draw a large yellow lightning bolt from the top corner of the face to the bottom corner.

3 Draw a second lightning bolt beside the first one.

**4** Dab glitter on the top and bottom of each lightning bolt, if you like.

**5** Use the makeup pencil or black paint to draw lines from the lightning bolts to the edge of the face.

**6** Paint thin red lips.

**7** Use hair gel to make hair stick straight out or tie it in lots of little pigtails, if you like.

## EASY COSTUME PIECES

- wacky sunglasses
- make antennae by attaching foil-covered balls or springs to the ends of pipe cleaners. Wrap the pipe cleaner ends around a headband.

# Fairy

*Sprinkle imaginary fairy dust
to grant wishes.*

## YOU WILL NEED

- white, red, blue, yellow and green face paints or face-painting crayons
- a black makeup pencil, paint or face-painting crayon
- glitter (optional)
- face-painting supplies (see pages 4 – 5)

1 Sponge a light layer of white on the whole face. Let the paint dry for three minutes.

2 Paint red lips.

3 Draw the outline of a cloud on the forehead with light blue (blend blue and white to make light blue).

4 Draw a curved red line on one cheek.

5 Draw an orange line next to it (blend red and yellow to make orange).

6 Add a yellow line next to the orange line, then green, then blue, then purple (blend red and blue to make purple).

7 Paint a red heart on the other cheek. Dab glitter on the heart, if you like.

8 Paint light blue on the eyelids.

## EASY COSTUME PIECES

- colorful ribbons for hair bows
- clothes in many colors
- a ballerina dress
- a silver wand made by gluing a cardboard star to a stick and covering everything with aluminum foil

# Easy designs

Paint these on your face, arms, hands, legs or feet. Draw the outline in black, then color in the shapes. You can make your own stencil. Trace your favorite shape onto a piece of cardboard, cut it out and paint around it.

## SKY

Paint stars, moons, planets and clouds to create a beautiful sky. You can add some glitter to make it sparkle.

## FLOWER

**1** Draw a small circle. Paint it yellow.

**2** Add five larger circles around the outside, each touching the middle circle.

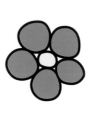

**3** Paint the larger circles blue.

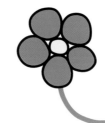

**4** Draw a green curved line down from the circles.

**5** Add green leaves to the stem by drawing half-moons.

## SCAR

1 Paint a white line.

2 Paint a red line next to it.

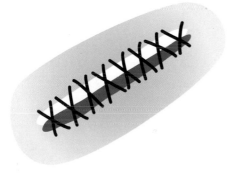

3 Use black paint or a makeup pencil to draw stitches (little x's) across the two lines.

## BALLOONS

1 Draw four long circles.

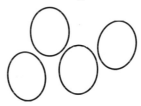

2 Draw a squiggly black line down from the bottom of each circle, connecting them at the bottom.

3 Draw a bow at the bottom to connect the lines.

4 Paint the balloons different colors.

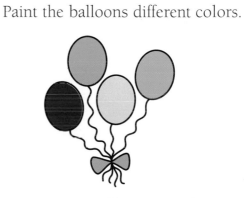

# More face-painting fun

- Act out fairy tales with your friends.
- Perform for a birthday party or family gathering.
- Volunteer to entertain at your school fun fair or local fundraiser.
- Set up a face-painting table at a garage sale, craft fair or picnic.
- Be a star at Halloween by painting the faces of other kids (and adults), and then lead them in a parade of characters.
- Tell jokes that fit your character, learn to juggle or try the simple magic trick on this page.

## MAKE A CLOWN BAND

- kazoos and whistles
- plastic containers filled with rice or dried beans for shakers
- pots and pans for drums

## ADD SOME MAGIC

Tightly roll up two sheets of newspaper. Tape the middle to keep the roll from coming apart.

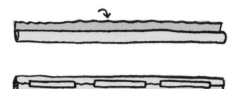

Cut halfway down the roll with scissors about six times.

Gently twist and pull up the very middle of the roll and — presto — a tree unfolds!